D1414226

Aspects of Primary Education

THE TEACHING AND LEARNING OF HISTORY AND GEOGRAPHY

London: Her Majesty's Stationery Office

© Crown copyright 1989
First published 1989

ISBN 0 11 270695 9

CONTENTS

SUMMARY

This publication, the fourth in a series of inspection reviews of primary education, reports and comments upon recent trends and issues in the teaching and learning of history and geography in primary schools.

The document describes standards currently achieved in these two subjects, identifies factors associated with good practice and discusses a number of issues for schools to consider with the implementation of the National Curriculum in mind.

We hope that the publication will be of interest, and helpful to those who are responsible for the planning, organisation and teaching of history and geography in primary schools, to teacher trainers and others concerned with primary education within and outside the maintained sector.

INTRODUCTION

1 This booklet discusses teaching and learning in what the HMI publication *The Curriculum from 5 to 16* calls 'the human and social' area of the curriculum. This, in the main, concerns the National Curriculum foundation subjects, history and geography. In the majority of English primary schools these subjects are taught as part of topic work which often also incorporates science, religious education, aspects of language development and art and design. These are dealt with elsewhere in the series and this booklet confines itself to history, geography and those aspects of topic work which involve those subjects.

2 The first section (page 7) describes briefly the situation in England as shown in the report of the National Primary Survey published in 1978. The second section (pages 8–14) sets out the findings of a monitoring exercise which involved the inspection of 285 primary schools between 1982 and 1986. The third section (pages 15–23) describes factors associated with good practice in these subjects, that emerged from a series of inspections made in the first half of 1988 to more than 50 schools where good practice had been identified. The fourth section (pages 24–29) considers some implications of this in the light of the implementation of the National Curriculum and identifies issues for schools to consider. The last section (pages 30–41) contains case studies which highlight and interrelate many of the characteristics of good practice.

History
and
Geography
in
the Mid-1970s:
The
findings
of
the
National
Primary
Survey

3. *Primary Education in England*, published in 1978, focused on the quality of education of pupils aged 7, 9 and 11 in 1,127 classes in 542 schools chosen to be representative of primary education in England. That report provides a useful baseline from which to analyse subsequent developments in the teaching of history and geography.

4. In most of the survey schools, history and geography were taught as parts of topic or thematic work, often in association with subjects such as religious education. They were both more firmly established in the curriculum of older children than that of younger ones.

5. Standards of work were generally unsatisfactory. In many classes where history and geography were taught, the work was judged to be superficial, repetitive and lacking in progression, often involving little more than copying from books. Only in a few classes were children developing an understanding of important concepts or acquiring essential skills.

6. A majority of the schools relied heavily on books and workcards to support the work in history with junior-aged children. Less than a half used television programmes. These were useful sources of information but it was relatively rare to find such programmes as part of well-planned schemes of work with thorough preparation and follow-up. Except in a few of the older classes, little use was made of artefacts, documents or sources of oral history. In geography a majority of the older pupils used atlases and slightly fewer used textbooks and workcards. Television and radio broadcasts, used in a few classes, helped children understand some of the features influencing people's lives.

7. Lack of adequate support and planning contributed to the unsatisfactory standards of work in both subjects. Only a small minority of schools had teachers with special responsibilities which included history or geography and only a similar proportion had schemes of work related specifically to those subjects.

Charting routes to local shops.

HISTORY AND GEOGRAPHY: MAIN FINDINGS FROM A NATIONAL MONITORING SURVEY 1982–86

8 During the period 1982–86, 285 schools were inspected as part of a national survey. They were selected according to their size, type and location to provide an illustrative sample of primary schools throughout England. A report was published on each school. In each case, judgements were made about the content and the quality of the pupils' work and about levels of attainment. As part of the inspection process HMI focused attention on specific aspects of the curriculum.

9 In the vast majority of the schools inspected history and geography were taught through the medium of topic or project work. Such topics frequently also included elements from science, language, religious education, art and craft, social studies, physical education, music and drama. In assessing the work of the schools through full inspections HMI made overall judgements of the effectiveness of topic work. Such work was considered reasonably satisfactory in a majority of the schools, including a small number where standards were particularly good. However, satisfactory or good practice was often related to aspects of topic work *other than* history and geography, for example science and language development. Inspection of the work related specifically to history and geography revealed a far less satisfactory picture in most, though not all, schools.

10 These findings showed that many schools had great difficulty in making satisfactory provision for history and geography within integrated work. It was clear, however, that some schools were able to combine knowledge, concepts and skills from a number of curriculum areas in order to enrich these subjects.

HISTORY

11 The standards of work achieved in history, whether taught separately or as part of topic work, were very disappointing. In only one in five infant schools and departments and one in three junior schools and departments were standards judged to be satisfactory or better.

12 In the majority of schools history was under-emphasised in the curriculum whether taught separately or, as in most cases, as part of topic work. In two out of three infant classes history received little or no attention. The situation was slightly better in junior-aged classes but even so history was under-emphasised or not taught in half the sample schools at the time of the inspection. Where a school gave due attention to history this tended to be reflected in quality of work at all ages.

13 Television and radio broadcasts prescribed the range and content of work in about two-thirds of classes. In many classes the absence of careful preparation and of adequate follow-up activities inhibited the profitable use of such stimuli and often meant that pupils' historical experiences were limited to acquiring unrelated factual information. This was especially true of children in infant and lower junior classes for whom teaching about the past was often confined to stories about dinosaurs, cavemen and the Romans.

What would we like in a new school?

14 Historical studies were based upon textbooks and commercially produced workcard series in a minority of schools. This over-reliance upon secondary sources enabled children to learn some historical facts but did not foster the development of historical skills.

16 The content of work was judged to be suitable in most or all aspects in just over a quarter of classes. Where content was judged as unsuitable this was usually because little attempt was made to relate it to the children's experience, it was based upon an uncritical choice of television

Old maps can be used to stimulate a wide variety of work.

15 In only a minority of the schools that were teaching history was learning based on the children's own experiences, their community or their immediate environment. Most of these schools used and benefited from visits to places of historical interest to support class-based work. Successful planning and follow-up to visits involved effective deployment of other historical resources such as artefacts, first-hand information, museum services and the memories of people known to the children. Often such activities were the basis for some positive links with other areas of the curriculum, such as aspects of children's language development or art and craft. These features occurred in a substantial number of schools although the integration of activities tended to do more to improve the range and quality of work in other areas of the curriculum than in history.

programmes or textbook series, or because it did little to develop historical skills such as evaluating primary sources or historical concepts such as time sequence and chronology; this was particularly the case in infant and lower junior classes. Appropriate content tended to be built upon first-hand experiences such as the use of visits and visitors, museum services, primary source material and artefacts to develop an evidence-based approach. In a large majority of the schools where the subject was being taught, local and English history (with an emphasis upon major figures and events) predominated. A few schools, usually situated in ethnically mixed areas, extended such studies to reflect and develop a world view of history.

17 Less than one-third of the schools in the survey had a teacher with responsibility for history although a further quarter had members of staff with oversight for areas such as topic work or environmental studies. Just over half of these teachers were responsible for preparing school guidelines, for acquiring and maintaining resources for historical work and for offering advice and support to their colleagues. There was very little specialist teaching in history or evidence of those with a specific curricular responsibility for the subject working alongside other teachers in their classes.

18   There was a tendency for the work in schools where there was a teacher with oversight for history to be rather better than the average. The subject qualifications of those with the responsibility made no difference to this relationship or to the emphasis given to history within the school. Although the overall influence of such teachers on the work of the school and of their colleagues was not strong there was a small number of instances where their influence led to certain historical concepts such as chronology, change and causality being better taught.

19   At its best, topic work facilitated the development of skills and understanding across a wide curricular range including historical studies. For example, in one school, three topics were chosen each year; efforts were made to ensure a balance between the historical, geographical and scientific elements and key concepts were identified and introduced through each topic in turn.

20   However, in most cases class teachers chose topics autonomously. This made it difficult to plan and monitor the systematic development of historical skills and understanding within individual topics and throughout the school. Topics frequently featured aspects of English history but often failed to extend these to the development of other perspectives, and were narrow in the range of skills they demanded, were unrelated to the children's experience and consisted of little more than

copying notes and illustrations. Unsurprisingly, work based on unco-ordinated planning by individual teachers was rarely successful in developing children's understanding as they progressed through the school, although opportunistic use of local or national festivals or anniversaries sometimes led to interesting work. For example, the celebration of Guy Fawkes Night and detailed study of the Gunpowder Plot stimulated discussions about the nature of loyalty and the responsibilities of friendship. There was some change during the period of the survey. Schools visited in the later stages were more likely to use the local environment to provide first-hand experiences for the study of historical concepts such as change.

21   Just over half the schools teaching history had written guidelines, but in only a quarter of the schools overall were the documents adequate or better and in only one in five did they have a significant influence on the quality of the work. Effective work in the development of historical skills, such as using and evaluating primary sources, and fostering the understanding of concepts, such as change and continuity, often reflected high-quality guidelines.

A traffic survey gave rise to ideas about road safety.

22 A large majority of schools had inadequate books, equipment and artefacts for historical studies. This reflects the low priority given to the subject. There was considerable evidence that high standards of work in history depended upon the adequate provision and effective use of a wide range of resources. For example, pupils in one junior school were involved in a study of 'My Town', the historical element of which was extensively exploited as a direct result of the collection and use of artefacts and photographs and of visits paid by people who remembered the old town. As part of the project the children studied nineteenth-century buildings, industry, clothing and transport. An extensive amount of material was collected for the topic and parents became involved in seeking information from birth and marriage certificates. To supplement their resources just over half the schools borrowed material from museum services. Where schools did obtain adequate resources for history, their use and effectiveness increased with the age of the child.

23 In almost all cases history was taught to mixed-ability classes. In some schools good quality curricular guidelines and influential teachers with oversight for history enabled staff to develop teaching styles and methods of classroom organisation suitable for such groupings. The best practice usually consisted of a range of approaches including teacher exposition, individual research, use of archive materials, artefacts, visits and visitors, discussion and oral work in groups. Drama was sometimes used successfully to enable children to understand something of the experiences of people from other times and to investigate events of the past. Poorer provision often emphasised the acquisition of knowledge without the development of understanding and made ineffective, excessive use of television and radio broadcasts. The quality of the teaching was invariably reflected in the pupils' standard of attainment in history.

24 Given the lack of guidance and a coherent policy in many schools it was not surprising that only about a fifth paid adequate attention to continuity and progression in the teaching of history.

25 In the vast majority of schools there were no records of pupils' progress in historical work. Some schools recorded the topics which pupils had studied but there were few examples of systematic attempts to identify individual responses to the work or to record children's progress in terms of increased knowledge, understanding and skills.

26 The picture of history and historical aspects of topic work revealed in this illustrative sample of schools (1982–86) was similar to that found by the National Primary Survey of almost a decade earlier. While more schools inspected in the early 1980s were aware of the need to incorporate aspects of history and were beginning to support its study through curricular documentation and leadership, standards of achievement remained low.

What was it like to wash clothes in 'the olden days'?

GEOGRAPHY

27 Overall standards of work in geography were very disappointing: in only one-quarter of both infant and junior schools and departments were they satisfactory or better. Though infrequent, good quality of work was more often reported for children of infant school age than for juniors. The situation improved somewhat over the course of the survey so that more of those schools inspected in the final year were teaching geography either separately or, more often, as an identifiable element of topic work.

28 Geography was most frequently taught in association with other areas of the curriculum and only occasionally as a separate subject, and then mainly to older classes. The amount of time allocated to work with a geographical component was rarely adequate and in a minority of schools there was either no or very little teaching of geography.

29 Where geography was taught through topic work in a coherent way it was usually relevant to the children. In most schools, however, there was a tendency for geography to lose its distinctive contribution and to become a vehicle for practising skills related to language and art. In contrast the mathematical and scientific potential of geographical skills, as in the case of map work and weather observations, was only occasionally exploited.

30 Within the schools the geographical topics frequently taught were farming, homes, weather, animals and transport. Children in approximately one-third of schools studied aspects of life in their own rural and urban communities; junior pupils were more likely to undertake such work. Pupils achieved satisfactory or better standards in map work, including the use of atlases and globes, in only a quarter of the schools. Junior pupils were more likely than infants to undertake work concerned with what places are like, how locations affect what people do and how people have used and adapted their surroundings. There was, however, clear evidence that even the youngest children were

capable of understanding these ideas at their own level.

31 In most schools children became involved at some stage with a range of activities concerning their own locality. Some of the best results were achieved where the work was of a practical nature and firmly based on the pupils' interests and experiences. For example, in the school where a pond study provided the starting-point for exploration of ideas in conservation and pollution, children displayed an understanding of the issues involved as well as seeking ways of resolving them. Towards the latter part of the survey a larger proportion of the schools were making effective use of the local environment as a stimulus for work of quality.

32 Work related to other places in the British Isles and the world was limited. The almost total absence of a national and world dimension to the work in many cases highlighted the need for schools to consider a broader perspective. This was achieved in one school where pupils were asked to plan a journey to different cities in England and abroad; they used previously acquired atlas skills with confidence to find places and determine the shortest routes between them. In a small minority of the schools geography was considered to be an effective vehicle for learning about cultural diversity. In one of these schools an attractive map of the world provided a focus for an annotated display, with children responding to the question 'Whereabouts in the world do we come from?'

33 One characteristic of schools with the highest standards of work was that pupils recorded their experiences in a variety of ways. They used illustrations, sketches, photographs, various forms of writing, art, three-dimensional craft and drama. In one school, a farm visit enabled the children to consolidate early ideas about dairy products by sorting and classify-

ing different artefacts and then making and tasting butter in the classroom. One class at another school made very good use of a variety of written modes which included geographically accurate entries for an imaginary diary based on Scott's last polar expedition.

34 About one-third of schools had a teacher with responsibility for geography, although, as indicated previously, a quarter had teachers with oversight of areas such as social studies, environmental studies or topic work. Where schools had a teacher with responsibility for geography there was often more effective continuity and progression within the subject. There was no link between initial teaching qualifications in geography amongst the staff and either the emphasis given to geography throughout the school or overall standards of achievement.

35 Over half of the teachers with responsibility for geography took the lead in preparing guidelines and in organising and purchasing resources. Their effect upon the quality of the work varied considerably but was often limited. However, there was some evidence that where teachers with special responsibility for the subject gave support and advice to other teachers, pupils' standards of achievement were higher.

36 In a few schools effective planning of content took into account the development of key geographical skills and ideas. However, there was rarely a clear rationale for the selection of topics, with little cognizance taken of the age, ability and experience of the pupils. Topics tended to be chosen in an idiosyncratic way by individual teachers, often determined by the television programmes that happened to be available at the time. There were more promising developments where well-considered guidelines were used to support staff with their planning.

37 There were written guidelines for geography in half the schools. Good quality schemes which had an appreciable influence on the work of the school were rare. The most effective explicitly identified key geographical skills, ideas and knowledge and provided guidance about teaching methods and classroom organisation.

38 The majority of schools had a barely adequate level of resources for geographical work; this reflects the under-emphasis given to the subject. In few schools did the resources reflect the multi-ethnic composition of either the school or society in terms of books, maps, audio and visual materials. There was some evidence to suggest that schools which were most successful in teaching geography also possessed a broad range of resources. Within these schools resources were well organised, carefully labelled and catalogued and easily accessible to staff and pupils. Such schools were more likely to have extensive central and class libraries, sometimes supplemented by local education authority (LEA) Schools Library Project collections; children were able to select appropriate materials with confidence and were accustomed to finding and using reference books in relation to particular topics. Some of the best work made good use of maps, globes, pictures and measuring equipment in addition to fiction and non-fiction books.

39 Half of the schools in the sample made some use of their grounds for environmental studies, most often in work related to science but, too often, the potential of such work was not exploited in a systematic way.

40 Nearly all the schools took their pupils on visits to support the curriculum and most children derived benefit from these. Such visits, usually within the immediate locality, gave rise to a variety of classroom activities. For example, one infant

school took its pupils on visits to the local park, farm, hospital, fire station, police station and city centre and every class project was supported by a range of visits and visitors. Standards of work improved considerably as a result of this whole-school policy.

41   Aspects of geography were usually taught to mixed-ability groups by the class teacher; specialist teaching was rare. Lessons were often over-directed and book-based with insufficient opportunities for pupils to express their own ideas or to engage in discussion with the teacher or among themselves. In those schools where the work was judged to be very good, children were responsible for their own learning to a marked degree and in one case made their own diagrammatic plans to show how their ideas could be developed. The highest standards of achievement were generally associated with problem-solving and investigative approaches and a combination of individual, group and class assignments. These were usually underpinned by relevant first-hand experiences which stimulated a range of interesting, practical activities.

42   Many schools found it difficult to provide continuity and progression. In only one-fifth were these features considered satisfactory or better.

43   The monitoring of children's progress was generally given insufficient attention; only one-fifth of schools maintained records. Although these records were usually summarised and made available to other staff, little or no effective use was made of them. In most cases the geography records comprised a list of topics covered by the class as a whole. A small minority of schools undertook a comprehensive assessment of what the children had actually learned and the range of skills acquired. Where this occurred the records were well used and contributed significantly to high achievement in the subject.

44   The National Primary Survey concluded that, although there was some good work, overall standards in geography were not satisfactory. While standards appear to have risen marginally, similar findings emerge from the inspections of the illustrative sample of schools undertaken between 1982 and 1986. There were, however, some areas of improvement. For example, the proportion of schools with a teacher with special responsibilities for this work rose from one-sixth to one-quarter, and the instances of written guidelines from one-third to one-half. These developments were extending the level of support and planning available but were not leading to significantly improved standards.

History and Geography Characteristics of Good Practice

45 In the first half of 1988 HMI visited, singly or in pairs, more than 50 primary schools throughout England, where good practice in history and geography had been identified either as a result of the 1982–86 illustrative survey or from routine contacts with schools. The characteristics described in this section are those which were observed during these visits and which were considered to be essential to work of quality and to pupils' understanding of historical and geographical ideas. The case studies presented below (pages 30–41) exemplify many of these factors, which apply equally across the primary age range.

A map showing ideas for a tourist trail beginning at the school and taking in places of interest.

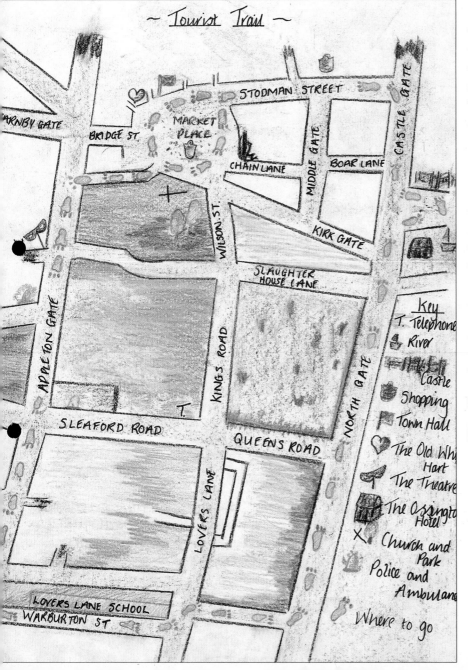

PLANNING AND ORGANISATION

46 Topic work was an important and integral part of the curriculum in all the schools where there was good practice; it was the major vehicle for promoting history, geography, science and, in many cases, several other subjects. The proportion of time devoted to topic work was at least one-fifth of that available, rising to three-quarters depending upon the number of curricular areas included, the nature of the topic undertaken and the interest levels and enthusiasm of the pupils. The more flexible the timetable, the easier it was for pupils to pursue and sustain their work in depth and to a satisfactory conclusion. In one school, for example, there was much evidence of sustained writing, detailed art work and problem-solving linked to model-making; pupils were able to concentrate on pieces of work for long periods of time, refining them from early drafts to finished products. The schools set out to achieve a **balance** both within and across the subjects which constituted topic work. During any one term or half a term there might be a focus upon one particular element such as history or geography, but other elements were not completely neglected within the topics being studied. Once the question of balance had been resolved the schools were better able to present pupils with a continuous range of experiences and build upon their previous knowledge. For example, one school gave great attention to the balance of the three main elements of history, geography and science, each element forming the core of an overall topic in one of the three terms each year.

47 An important factor in the successful planning and teaching of this area of the curriculum was the carefully considered use of good, comprehensive **documentation**. The most effective guidelines were those which helped the schools achieve a consistency of approach, style of learning and organisation, thus enabling the work to develop progressively.

15

They were usually produced in consultation with the staff and took into account previous and subsequent phases of schooling. They were characterised by a clarity of aims and the identification of teaching objectives in terms of the knowledge, understanding, skills and attitudes to be advanced through studying history and geography throughout the age range of the school. Guidance on the use of resources, well-planned first-hand experiences and advice on methodology and classroom organisation were other features of the best guidelines.

48 There was a clear association between the quality of pupils' work and the thoroughness of **planning** by the teacher. Effective planning invariably gave attention to the elements of learning: knowledge, understanding, skills and attitudes, to the teaching methods and to the available resources. A consistent approach to planning throughout the whole school had a unifying influence, helped to avoid unnecessary repetition of content and gave significant support to individuals, or teams of teachers. In one school preparation for a topic began with a full staff meeting where a theme for the term was agreed, taking into account the need for a balanced and sequential range of experiences over a year. Following a brainstorming session a list of suggested activities for each year group was produced under different subject headings and these were cross-referenced, for example, to relate skills and inform understanding where different learning experiences shed light on a similar concept. At another school, teachers' plans of past themes were retained and located centrally as a record of work completed by each class and used to plan future topics.

49 **Continuity** through the school in terms of time allocation, organisation and general themes was achieved more effectively than **progression** in skills and concepts of the subject areas constituting a topic. The **monitoring** of individual children's progress based upon **assessment** of their understanding helped teachers to determine what pupils needed to know and understand and the type of provision necessary to meet those needs. In one large infant school there was a discernible development in the skill of map-making from the reception to the top infant classes; detailed plans of the classroom drawn by the older children had developed from reception class experiences including the drawing of pupils' homes and bedrooms.

50 A teacher on the main scale, with or without an allowance payment, was usually given responsibility for the **oversight and co-ordination** of topics within the schools. The most effective co-ordinators adopted a variety of strategies in order to influence positively the quality of work throughout the school. These included writing or reviewing guidelines, teaching as a specialist, working alongside colleagues, giving advice on planning, purchasing and organising resources and leading staff meetings held to discuss issues connected with the development of work in history and geography whether it was organised through topics or otherwise.

51 The heads of schools where there was good practice usually had a range of **leadership** characteristics including a management style which encouraged a collegial approach to curricular development and a clear view of the aims and purposes of historical and geographical aspects of the curriculum. They made their regard for the importance of these subjects plain and were able to engage class teachers in an assessment of studies in progress in the context of the work of the school as a whole.

TEACHING AND LEARNING

52 Two highly important characteristics of effective learning in these subjects were good quality **discussion** and **questioning** generated by the teacher. An essential element within these

exchanges was the pitch of the teaching in relation to the levels of understanding displayed by the pupils. Discussion often started from the children's own knowledge with the teachers prompting new facts and ideas. The teachers' questions often encouraged children to recall and reflect upon evidence from their reading, from first-hand experience, or, sometimes, from personal research done at home. For example, in one project on building materials the children showed considerable understanding and knowledge as a result of discussing the project with their parents. In effective work teachers maintained a balance between asking questions and giving information. The most effective questioning allowed time for the children to consider their responses and also to ask their own questions. The work was planned around a series of interesting focal points so that the children's interest was sustained and they were motivated to extend their learning.

Microcomputers are a valuable aid to history and geography.

53 Children worked in a variety of ways, individually, in small or large groups or as a member of the whole class. **Grouping** was planned according to the nature of the tasks and to make the best use of resources such as computers, films or primary source materials. These arrangements generated a great deal of debate and discussion and helped the children to become closely involved in the development of

the topic. For the most part **styles of learning** were open and investigative; children used primary sources of evidence such as buildings and land sites, photographs and authentic printed material from archives and museum collections; the teachers played important roles in guiding their pupils' learning, progressively, through the use of such materials.

54 Historical or geographical studies were often planned to incorporate people, places, events or things that were familiar to the pupils. By this means the children proceeded **from the known to the unknown** so extending the range of what they knew, understood and were able to do. For example, in history, some teachers attempted to achieve a balance between family history, local studies, British and world history and to ensure that the selections developed a knowledge of chronology. In geography, some pupils studied similarities and differences between their local area and more distant places both in this country and abroad.

55 Basic **concepts and skills** identified by the teachers were specifically incorporated into the work. The notion of cause and effect, for example, was a means by which children in one school began to identify relationships between events in the past and the present; they used census and archive material to study the effects of mine closures and technological developments on employment patterns. In many of the schools ideas of seasonal change, location, distance, direction, the influence of environmental conditions on people's lives and the interdependence of communities were systematically developed. In one class a study of weather patterns involved the pupils in discussions about measuring the wind speed, rainfall, temperature and sunshine in order to record seasonal differences. The children made and used simple equipment and produced records to compare conditions observed. In another school the nature of evidence was examined through a

comparison of news items in newspapers and magazines; this evidence was considered in terms of reliability and possible alternative interpretations.

56 Many topics also included a range of **ideas** which related closely, though not exclusively, to history and geography. Communication, for example, was studied using art, craft, information technology, discussion and writing. Ideas arose as offshoots of a topic or as a way of initiating work. A topic on life in polar regions included ideas on exploration, animal life and testing the insulative properties of materials. The best results were achieved when pupils were helped explicitly to understand the relationships between such ideas.

57 In many of the schools children were encouraged to develop their appreciation of **what it might be like to be someone else** in a particular situation. In one example children handled flints and other artefacts in their study of the lifestyle of early man. A second group identified the route followed by Charles Darwin in HMS *Beagle*, using atlases and Mercator projection maps; they read about living conditions on board, the type of food eaten, the speed of the ships and the distance travelled. The best work occurred when clear, accurate historical and/or geographical background information was presented to the children.

58 The acquisition and development of specific skills was seen as a very important part of the work. A key historical skill of using the vocabulary and conventions of **chronology** was often approached through local, national or international studies. Pupils acquired a sense of time by creating personal time lines which involved studying changes during the first 10 years of their life or their immediate family's history. Another major skill fostered was the ability to ask **historical questions** such as 'What were the similarities and differences between then and now?' and 'How

do we know?' in order to develop a sense of **change and continuity**. Children engaged in a village study applied the following questions to census and other data: 'Why are there fewer people in the village today than in 1951?'; 'What kind of different jobs might people do today and are any jobs the same as 100 years ago?' In one school children experimented with soil samples to **identify** the constituent parts and **determine** the rate of drainage; they devised an **experiment** to show the presence of pockets of air in the soil; the teacher, through questioning and discussion, linked the classroom activities with the world of farming and market gardening.

59 The progression from the early stages of drawing simple **plans and maps** to the use of more complex plans and maps of varying scale was a gradual process in many of the schools. Other skills such as the use of symbols, directional compasses, map keys and route selection, measuring distance and scaling up and down were developed as the children communicated their findings and ideas through writing, pictures, models, diagrams and maps.

60 Several aspects of the **local environment** were studied. These could be the site and the grounds of the school itself, or the immediate locality and its features or locations of particular interest further afield. Frequently historical and/or geographical studies were made of the village, town, local church or the school. Some schools sought to improve the educational potential of their site by planting young trees, herb gardens or plots using different soil types; by creating nature trails, ponds or wild areas; or by building weather stations, nesting boxes and bird feeding tables. The use of such facilities helped children to develop **research skills** such as the accurate **collection** and **classification** of information. In many cases museums, art galleries, industrial sites, field study centres, country parks, castles and churches were visited by schools to stimulate historical and geographical studies. For example, one class made particularly good use of local shops, building sites, a disused railway line and farm houses when researching the question, 'What was this area like 10 years ago?' In this way the environment became both an important subject for study and a powerful resource for the development of a range of skills.

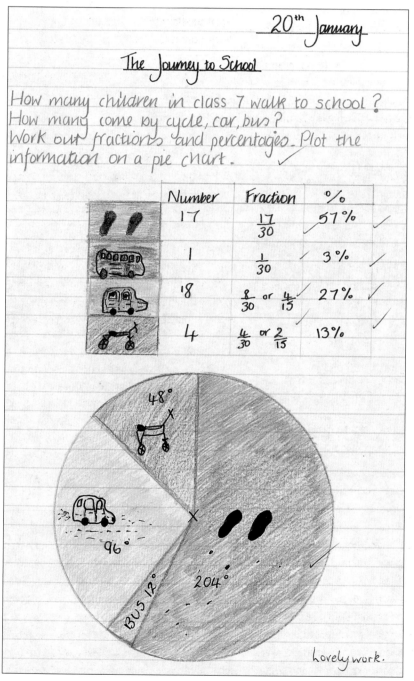

Different ways of presenting information about how children journey to school.

61 A **visit** to a place of interest further afield frequently gave rise to successful learning, serving either as a stimulus for further study or the final stage of research. One school visited a sorting office as part of a topic on the postal service and used this experience for a variety of activities including the development of geographical skills and knowledge as the children planned routes for postmen. Such visits provided first-hand, practical experiences for the children and contact with adults with specialist knowledge. The purposes of the visits were clearly identified and due regard was paid to the children's safety; preparation was thorough so that children were well aware of what they were to do and of the necessary background information; follow-up activities were equally well planned. Some schools undertook residential visits which brought important social as well as educational benefits.

62 Schools using a topic approach usually did so in order to integrate or bring together ideas and methods of enquiry from a variety of subject perspectives. As well as being the means for teaching history and geography many schools saw topic work as a powerful vehicle for the development of a variety of **language skills**. The most effective written work was produced where a variety of styles was used and pupils were encouraged to correct and re-draft their efforts. Reading primary sources and reference books and presenting the results of such research were important ways of applying and improving basic communication skills. Many schools used novels associated with themes being studied in order to illustrate some of the main strands of their enquiry. Thus, in one class, selections of children's literature dealing with the experiences of people from a variety of backgrounds were used as part of an historical study of the Second World War. The use of literature was also a powerful stimulus for personal writing. One group of children studying the Edwardian period produced po-

etry, anecdotes and sketches in the style of *The Diary of an Edwardian Lady*. Oral skills were enhanced by discussions arising from successful investigations and by drama.

63 As pupils recorded and presented the results of their studies there were many opportunities for **artistic** and other **creative** forms of expression; indeed the best quality work often incorporated varied visual forms of presentation including photography. **Musical** experiences were included in the work of one class studying Elizabethan life as they compared instruments from that period with those of today, learnt and played contemporary tunes and practised court dances. **Mathematical** activities formed a major part of many topics; a study of paper, for example, enabled pupils to report their results using a variety of graphical forms and to make detailed predictions about the amount of paper the school would use over a period of time. **Craft, design and technology** was integrated into the topic of one class which designed, built and tested a variety of bridge structures and arrived at a valid conclusion about the relative strengths of different constructions.

RECORDING AND ASSESSMENT

64 Teachers usually recorded the topics undertaken with their classes, most frequently in terms of broad themes rather than specific skills, concepts and attitudes. These **records** were passed on from class to class, thus helping to avoid repetition and forming a useful check-list both for the range of topics covered and the balance of the constituent elements. However, they were not used for recording the development of skills, concepts and attitudes. One school had prepared detailed **evaluation** sheets on which each class teacher wrote a termly critique of the development of the topics studied; these were cross-referenced to a planning sheet which identified specific skills and ideas with the aim of making teaching in this area of the curriculum more effective throughout the school. A comprehensive **monitoring** procedure at another school included a simple grid to note the development of the skills of observation, classification, measurement, investigation and information across the three major areas of the curriculum associated with topic work; this chart, together with the plans that supported the work in individual classes, enabled teachers to decide which activities of work would be needed to support the future learning of skills.

65 In most schools **assessment** was related specifically to the extent to which children had produced work at an appropriate level. Comments and suggestions for the development of work were usually made on this assessment. Sometimes individual work of quality was passed on to the next teacher as a record of successful achievement. In some classes the pupils themselves were involved in helping to keep a record of class activities; this proved an effective strategy. Children's own work was sometimes used as a record of achievement and there was usually space on a child's general record sheet for teachers to make comments about topic work. However, there was scope even in the best schools to improve and extend monitoring procedures so that an individual pupil's acquisition of the range of skills and knowledge to be learnt through topics could be charted.

RESOURCES FOR LEARNING

66 The most common resource was **books** which were carefully selected for the pupils' levels of interest and ability and were readily accessible; the extra support given through **School Library Services** and the provision of topic collections was an important part of the overall planning. Other **printed materials** such as census returns, parish registers, log books, photographs, diagrams, charts and maps were well used, particularly when focused on selected areas of study. A village study by one primary school made good use of printed resources, together with regular visits to the village and the support of the County Records Office and the National Trust. Characteristics of good resource management included a simple, logical classification system for books and **audio-visual aids** which were well catalogued and stored in ways that encouraged pupils to make their own selection for particular assignments. Resources were most effectively used where there was detailed planning.

A chart showing the movement of traffic in different directions around the school.

67 **Educational broadcasts** were used to initiate or support many studies. Where these were used selectively and with carefully planned preparatory and follow-up activities they were able to provide information not otherwise available in the classroom and in a form likely to appeal to pupils. One school used episodes from an educational television series to illustrate and emphasise points about life in Edwardian times. Where schools had **video** facilities they were able to record programmes for later transmission or show selected parts, thereby introducing an important element of flexibil-

ity. **Photography** provided good resources for some children. One school with a range of cameras used slides and photographs as resources for learning, to stimulate further discussion and to record work completed. Another used a video camera to record effectively the development of an environmental project.

68 **Information technology** was used in a variety of ways to extend the range and depth of studies in this area of the curriculum. For example, programs for the **storage and retrieval** of information enabled pupils to handle complex data in a manageable format and gave them experience of working with modern technology. **Word-processing** facilities gave children experience of composing, editing and re-drafting accounts of the results of their investigations. Such programs were sometimes also part of the enquiry. For example, a school entered material from an 1823 newspaper and compared the contents and styles of writing with those of a modern publication. **Control technology** was also used: one class researching a topic on waste disposal used a computer, an interface and commercially produced technical equipment to design and make a conveyor belt for the transportation and sorting of refuse. Other ways in which information technology was applied to topic work included **concept keyboards**; **simulations** which taught children about life in other times and other places and presented them with some of the problems inherent in those life styles; and **instructional programs** which helped children acquire knowledge of mapping symbols.

69 **Museums, art galleries and libraries** provided valuable support to schools. Some informed the schools of projected exhibitions and this assisted planning; loan collections of materials, sometimes selected by the school and museum staff, enhanced the displays. In one local authority the history adviser in association with a museum had produced a series of 'time boxes' each representing a specific time span and containing several artefacts from that period. Children were encouraged to contribute to this collection of resources through their own observations and research. They created materials such as video films, records, writing, drawing and taped interviews.

70 Classroom **display** served a variety of purposes including demonstrating to parents, staff and the pupils themselves the range and quality of work that the children were doing. It also provided a focus for the learning taking place and gave encouragement for further enquiry and investigation. Many effective displays reflected the careful thought given to the balance between children's own work, printed materials and artefacts. In a reception class a display of old and new artefacts was planned as a starting-point for a topic; it stimulated discussion and helped the children to think about ideas of change and continuity. A collection of herbs accompanied by information books and charts in a junior classroom encouraged discussion, writing and investigation about herbs in Tudor times and those used now. A collection or Ordnance Survey maps in another school was displayed alongside maps of the same area dating back to the eighteenth century. Samples of rock were displayed and linked to areas of the terrain where they might be found. Through captions a range of questions was presented to the observer with occasional references to specific books.

71 Many of the displays reflected the observations, ingenuity and resourcefulness of the children. The quality of presentation of both individual and collaborative pieces of work depended to a high degree on teachers' expectations. In one school, celebrating its fiftieth anniversary, children collected photographs, newspaper cuttings and school reports of parents and grandparents and tape-recorded their memories; these were displayed with their stories and pictures alongside school log books and official forms. In another the children brought together an impressive collection of their local discoveries including old farm machinery, tools and household and industrial implements. In one infant class pictograms illustrated the different types of houses occupied by the children, and there were detailed sketches of houses observed on visits. A frieze of the story of 'The Three Little Pigs' included a collection of different building materials which stimulated further activities. On the floor of the classroom a model of a town showed houses, shops and a road system. The domestic play area was a hardware shop with items colour-coded and priced.

72 **Visitors** to the schools were used either as sources of specialist knowledge or to illustrate ideas or themes being investigated by the children. For example, a mother took a baby into school to help with a topic on change; pupils were able to consider the rate and nature of the growth that occurs during their life-span. In many cases old people were invited into schools to talk about their memories of life in earlier days, at school, at work or during the war. These proved to be powerful sources of information for children researching local or family history and helped them acquire a sense of chronology and an understanding of life in other times. Those with specialist knowledge such as museum liaison officers were also effective especially when they brought artefacts or exhibits that children could touch, when workshop sessions were organised or when follow-up activities were carefully planned.

73 Much good work was supported by the interest and involvement of the **families** of pupils. As well as offering general encouragement parents and grandparents often helped by providing information or artefacts relevant to topics or by bringing specialist knowledge, skills or interests to the classroom. One school asked parents with computing skills to help with the analysis of census information, while another school invited parents with creative skills to assist the pupils to present their findings in an attractive way. Those parents with interesting experiences to relate provided new information or insights for children to consider. For example, one class heard of the travels of a parent who had visited China. Some valuable follow-up activities resulted from the vivid account. Field trips and residential work could often proceed only with the voluntary involvement of parents who helped with supervision. Other members of the community were also involved. For example, one school governor provided information about Australia which resulted in pen-friendships being formed. In another school a dinner lady told of her experiences of working in a cotton mill. Local authors, artists and those from other occupations sometimes came into school to talk about their work. One school regularly invited a local farmer to talk about the farming year.

74   Good practice in history, geography and topic work was supported by a number of **LEA advisers**. Some of these had an authority-wide responsibility for a subject area such as history or geography or for areas of experience such as environmental studies. They helped individual schools by providing additional resources and guidance on projects and they worked with teachers on the development of LEA or local schemes of work. **Advisory teachers** with a subject-specific responsibility or a more general role made valuable contributions to the work of some schools. Members of teams such as the Environmental Education team, the Rural Studies Centre, the Museum Support Services, Health Education Services and the staff of Nature Reserves also supported project work in schools. Good planning enabled one class on a visit to an exhibition to meet 'a rich Victorian lady writer' (a teacher from the gallery) who invited them to choose a picture for her to write about. The children enthusiastically wrote their own stories as a follow-up exercise to this initial stimulus.

Producing a cross-section of a hill from a contour map.

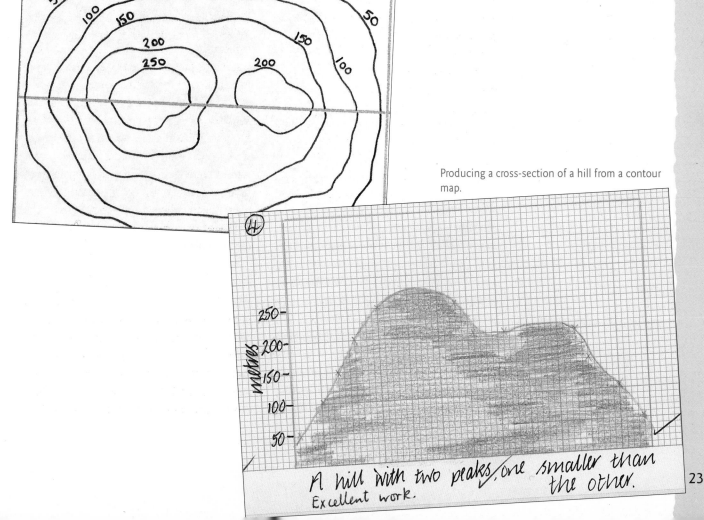

23

75 Previous sections have shown that most primary schools do not provide challenging historical and geographical work for their pupils. In too many schools, too little time is devoted to these subjects; they are poorly planned and taught, and assessment is superficial or non-existent. Some schools, however, achieve a great deal in these areas and the case studies presented below (pages 30–41) set out some of the characteristics of such work. This section identifies and, through reference to the case studies, illustrates a series of issues which schools need to consider as they seek to plan and implement work of good quality in history and geography in the light of the National Curriculum.

76 A major issue concerns the way in which history and geography are to be **organised within the curriculum**. As a result of the preparation for the National Curriculum schools will have clear direction on what should constitute the primary curriculum. After attainment targets and programmes of study for history and geography have been determined much will still be left for the schools themselves to decide. It needs to be remembered that although the National Curriculum is described in subject terms there is no requirement for it to be taught in this way. Schools still need therefore to decide the degree to which they will concentrate on teaching history and geography separately, integrate these studies or include them in a broader range of topic work. The evidence presented in this document has shown that, while most schools teach history and geography through topic work, much of the best practice occurs when such an approach involves a detailed study which is predominantly historical or geographical in nature rather than integrating several subjects around some general theme. However schools decide to organise this area of the curriculum there will have to be clearly identifiable historical and geographical studies, as these terms are commonly understood, in a manner which meets the requirements of programmes of study and attainment targets. The HMI publications in the Curriculum Matters series *Geography from 5 to 16* and *History from 5 to 16* suggest the knowledge, concepts, skills and attitudes that such studies might contain.

77 Schools should also consider the contribution that history and geography can make through their **links with core and other foundation subjects**. Effective work in these subjects inevitably enriches language development, for example, through the variety of oral and written material that pupils encounter as they study historical and geographical subject matter. The understanding of important mathematical and scientific ideas is often well supported by work in history and geography which may also be linked to non-foundation subjects such as social studies, often the focus of interest and study with younger primary children. History and geography deal with a wide range of human experience; it is important that their potential for the teaching of **cross-curricular themes** is explored. For instance, teaching about issues of equal opportunities or environmental education, and their influence upon individuals and groups, can act as unifying themes in pupils' historical and geographical studies.

78 Successful work in this area of the curriculum requires a clear understanding of what the teaching needs to encompass matched by a similar clarity of how it is to be organised and managed. The schools in the three case studies below took an integrative approach describing this aspect of their work as topics in two instances and environmental studies in the other. However, in each case there was **a clear understanding of the distinctive contribution that history and geography can make to children's learning**. In the first case study the historical perspective was very strong with the class teacher clearly identifying the nature of the historical questions to be posed to, and by, the children and the historical skills and concepts which they would need to develop in order to be able to answer these. This historical work was not seen as an end in itself but led on to a wide variety of studies in other areas of the curriculum. In the other two case studies the major focus was geographical and again a clear analysis had been made of what important geographical knowledge, skills and concepts could contribute to the pupils' total educational experience.

79 Once there has been such an analysis it becomes possible to consider the **balance of experience** that schools wish pupils to have over a set period of time, such as half a term, a term, a year or a Key Stage in the National Curriculum. A problem encountered by many schools is that the work can easily become fragmented irrespective of whether it is taught through topics or mainly as single subjects. It is therefore essential to plan the work as thoroughly as possible. Coherence is often best achieved where greater emphasis is given to either history or geography for a given period of time so as to attain a balance over a term or a year. Such a strategy is usually more successful than tackling aspects of both subjects through a weekly timetable. If the work is planned on a longer timescale extended investigations of the kind described in the case studies become possible. While it is for the school to decide what amount of time needs to be devoted to these studies the attainment targets for history and geography in the National Curriculum will inevitably influence that decision as practice proves what is possible.

80 Teachers will also need to consider the **balance to be achieved between the knowledge, understanding and skills required** for each Key Stage as the work progresses. It could be argued, with some justification, that the children in the case study schools spent a lot of time developing a range of historical and geographical skills and concepts but only applied these to a limited amount of subject matter. The charge, in the past, has been that children often leave primary schools with well-developed skills in history and geography but knowing about little beyond their immediate locality. The attainment targets and programmes of study should be of considerable help to schools in identifying the knowledge that children should acquire during each of the Key Stages and in achieving an effective balance between the development of understanding and of appropriate skills. However, much will depend on how well the attainment targets and programmes of study are incorporated into more **detailed schemes of work**. In the second case study the staff had together decided a policy which identified those skills and concepts to be introduced and developed in each year's work. Such an approach allows for **progression** in the children's work. As pupils acquire knowledge and skills they are able to use these for more advanced study. Reports and surveys by HMI have consistently noted insufficient progression in history and geography. This aspect is another where programmes of study developed as part of the implementation of the National Curriculum should be of considerable help to primary schools.

81 Similar points can be made regarding **continuity**. Inspection reports and surveys have regularly found unnecessary repetition and omissions in this area of the curriculum. Continuity can be enhanced if a school identifies which subject matter will be studied in each term or year. Again, the programmes of study will give guidance here. Many schools, particularly those advocating a topic work approach, quite reasonably wish to be able to respond to local or national events or topical issues or engage in intensive projects in a way which cannot be repeated. For example, the class teacher in the first case study would be unlikely to wish to spend as much time on the same investigation with another class and, indeed, it was the uniqueness of the enquiry which enabled it to be sustained over a long period and which motivated the children. In such cases, schools need to develop strategies which will allow them to **monitor** what children work on in order to avoid the problems of repetition or the omission of important items.

82 History and geography are foundation subjects of the National Curriculum and, as such, have to be taught to pupils for a reasonable **amount of time** in advance of the attainment targets and programmes of study coming into force. Underemphasis has been given to these areas of the curriculum, particularly for children in Key Stage 1. The evidence from full inspections of primary schools supports the view that the youngest pupils are capable of understanding what have been traditionally regarded by many teachers as quite difficult historical and geographical ideas. It is increasingly apparent that, for example, ideas associated with change, chronology, location and distribution can be understood by young children at an appropriate level if experienced in a practical way and within a context which makes sense to them. Schools, therefore, need to consider how best to ensure that children have **continuous experience** of history and geography throughout the full age range. This would also go some way towards overcoming the difficulties encountered in trying to negotiate a **liaison** between primary and secondary school provision. National Curriculum programmes of study will help ensure that there is liaison in subject matter but continuity of approach can only be achieved if the primary school itself has developed a coherent policy for teaching and learning in these subjects.

83 Another aspect of provision in history and geography which many schools find particularly difficult is **differentiation**. The third case study describes how a small rural school was able to identify tasks for children of different ages and ability within mixed-aged classes as part of a school-wide environmental studies approach. Similarly the first case study shows how the same resource – census material – can be used in a way appropriate for different ability levels within the same class. Here it was the skill of the class teacher which enabled all the pupils to be given challenging activities to complete. However, this issue is one that is best dealt with by deciding upon a school-wide policy rather than leaving it only to individual teachers. Attainment targets for history and geography should prove particularly useful for teachers aiming to match pupils' work to their stage of development and capabilities.

84 The three case studies describe schools of different sizes. The number of teachers in a school can often be a crucial factor in deciding how history and geography are planned and taught. In each of the case study schools strong **leadership** was vital to successful work in this area of the curriculum. In two cases this was provided by the head, in the other by a teacher with specific curricular responsibility under the guidance of the head. In all the schools this influence was sufficient to support good practice in classes other than that of the person with responsibility. It is important that there is a member of staff who takes a leading role in developing work in historical and geographical studies. This may be the head or a teacher designated as a curriculum leader, a consultant or a co-ordinator. The title is not important, the function is. It is essential that the individual with responsibility has the authority to ensure that curriculum planning proceeds in a co-ordinated way with all members of staff being involved; that documentation supports and extends the work of colleagues; that models of good practice are provided by the curriculum leader's own classroom; that resources are organised in such a way as to be accessible and appropriate to the children; and that the topics studied are monitored and the children's work assessed in a consistent way.

The curriculum leader's support can also be exercised through consultancy: by offering advice and specialised knowledge; by engaging in team or paired teaching in order to explore the possibilities of different teaching styles; or by doing some specialist teaching where appropriate.

85 Surveys have shown that there are considerable numbers of teachers whose **expertise and qualifications** in history and geography are not being used. It is important that schools should identify such expertise and deploy it to best advantage. As in all areas of the curriculum the teaching of history and geography can-

not be left solely as the responsibility of the class teacher. Leadership and support are essential if standards are to improve.

86 The strength of the work described in the three case studies reflects a great deal of **professional skill and experience**. In each case these are the results not only of the initial training and the personal interest and ability of the teachers involved but also of programmes of **professional development**. These include support and advice from LEA personnel, in-service courses and workshop experiences. Sometimes staff development can occur within schools and can be serviced by the resources of the school itself but in other instances external support is needed. School staffs need to analyse the extent and the levels of their own expertise and experience in history and geography, identify appropriate in-service needs and seek to meet these from the variety of sources available under LEA training grants schemes and other local and national initiatives.

87 In each of the three case study schools the acquisition and use of **resources** to support work in history and geography had been a priority. Particular emphasis was placed on those resources which would give children first-hand experiences within whatever topic was being studied. Some of these resources were already part of the immediate environment. Others had to be acquired specifically for the children to study and use such as local parish records, historical artefacts or maps of a particular area. Sometimes these had to be put into a form that made them more accessible to the pupils as in the storing of census material on a computer fact file. Another key feature was the way in which resources were associated with the development of specific concepts or skills. For example, the concept of continuity and change was illustrated, in the first case study, by the use of artefacts; and the skills of map-making became relevant when associated with the study of the school grounds in the second case study. Such a relationship

Using different scales to show the location of 'my house'.

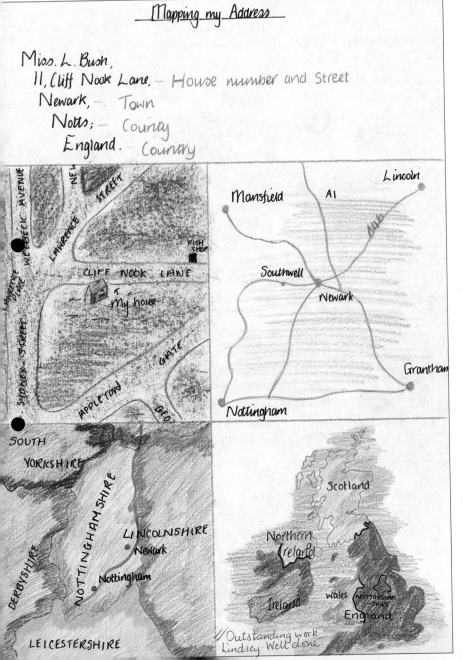

27

between historical and geographical knowledge and skills and the resources that can be used to help pupils acquire these is only possible if teachers have a clear idea of what specifically they intend that their pupils should learn. They should also know what experiences they wish their pupils to have that may produce unplanned but valuable learning across a wider range of subject matter. Both types of learning outcomes depend upon clear intentions on the part of the teacher and these make sound decisions about resource provision and development easier to make.

88 It is not uncommon to find schools with resources which are poorly matched to the curriculum and which are located in such a way as to make access difficult. The National Curriculum should prompt schools to consider the possibilities offered by existing materials; whether or not these are as accessible as they might be to both teachers and pupils; whether they are used as much as they might be and what else is required in order to attain historical and geographical aims and objectives. When considering these issues the potential of **modern technology** should be harnessed. The contribution of information technology, control technology and photographic and video cameras was particularly noticeable in the high quality work described in the case studies. Again teachers might like to consider their use of newer technologies and, where necessary, seek help in acquiring and developing skills in their use.

89 Aspects of the teaching of history and geography which primary schools often find particularly difficult are those of **assessment and record-keeping**. When attainment targets and programmes of study are produced for these two subjects, schools will have a clear idea of the goals towards which their pupils are working. Similarly, the assessment arrangements that will be developed through the work of the Schools Examination and Assessment

Council (SEAC) as part of the implementation of the National Curriculum will give indications of the principles upon which teachers should assess children's progress and attainment and the methods by which this should be done. Assessment should provide teachers with information about the historical and geographical knowledge, understanding and skills that pupils have and about learning difficulties they are facing so that the next series of activities can be planned more effectively. It is not enough merely to record the activities that pupils have completed.

90 It is important to link assessment to the teaching and learning which is occurring and has occurred in the classroom. Any forms of assessment used should take account of the manner by which the study of history and geography is organised within the school. Thus, if separate subjects are taught then continuous class-based assessment will need to be based upon that approach. If topic work is used then this too will need to be reflected in the assessment procedures that are used. In either case assessment should be concerned with the content of the studies that the pupils have undertaken and be clearly linked to whatever knowledge, concepts and skills have been developed during the Key Stage. Continuous assessment of class work will play an important role and this will be aided by a clear identification of the underlying targets and an analysis of the various elements which go to make up work in history and geography. The **moderation** of teacher assessments by other teachers should prove a useful means by which staff can develop their assessment skills and refine their understanding and interpretation of learning in these subjects.

91 An important factor of the successful work described in the three case studies was the importance that was placed upon the **evaluation**, by teachers and pupils alike, of work in progress and that which had been completed. In the

first case study this took the form of written accounts placed in workbooks produced by the class. In the second case study each teacher wrote regular critiques of the topic work in his or her class and this was seen as an invaluable aid to curriculum development. Schools should consider how they might evaluate their own work in these aspects of the curriculum and use the results to make their teaching more effective.

92 History and geography have been identified as parts of the National Curriculum which all pupils in maintained schools should receive. Although many teachers recognise the contribution which these subjects can make to the education of their pupils and some succeed in providing historical and geographical education of quality, the picture revealed by national monitoring is a disappointing one. It is intended that this booklet should help the staffs of schools as they consider how to improve standards in these important aspects of the curriculum.

GOOD
PRACTICE
OBSERVED:
THREE
CASE
STUDIES

The following case studies exemplify many of the characteristics of good practice described in the previous section. They include work in infant and junior classrooms in 1988 and have been chosen to illustrate how many of the factors associated with sound work in history and geography were interrelated in practice. Following a review of their current provision, schools should consider what steps, if any, need to be taken to make progress towards the incorporation of those elements of good practice that are identified in the case studies.

CASE STUDY 1

93   The school is located in an area closely associated with the development of the Industrial Revolution and near to several important sites of industrial archaeological interest. It is a county junior school with over 200 pupils on roll. The semi-open-plan design is well used to aid the development of the enquiry-based work to which the school is committed. The school serves a housing estate where adult unemployment is higher than the national average.

94   A teacher has oversight of topic work throughout the school and her responsibilities include updating documentation for this area of the curriculum and maintaining a resource base of appropriate documents, leaflets, pamphlets and information about places from which artefacts may be borrowed. She also undertakes the dissemination of good practice by displaying children's work throughout the school.

95   The school's guidelines are closely based upon the Schools Council Project 'History, Geography and Social Science 8–13 (Man in Time, Place and Society)'. They clearly indicate those skills and concepts which it is hoped will be developed through topic work during the four years that the children are at the school. The teachers are required to submit plans to the head before such studies are undertaken.

These usually take the form of a flow chart or a web which indicates the skills and knowledge to be covered. It is expected that topics studied in any one year will vary in emphasis with each term's work paying particular attention to history, geography or science. This approach is understood and followed by all members of staff.

96   In the year 6 class of 27 pupils, where the focus was mainly historical, the aim was to use available evidence and primary resource material to investigate a question of genuine historical concern: an abandoned local lead mining village where a disused school building was used to begin an investigation into the life of the village and the reasons for its decline.

97   Planning by the class teacher took the form of the identification of key resources that would be used by the children in their investigation. In addition consideration was given to those historical skills and concepts which could be developed by such a study. These included:

•   the examination of a range of historical evidence;

•   the asking of historical questions;

•   the nature of change as it had affected this village between 1881 and the present day;

•   historical cause and effect as evidenced by the decline of lead mining in the area;

•   the ability to draw inferences from small, unrelated pieces of historical information.

Pupils posed a historical question during a visit to an abandoned village.

The second clue was an examination of two maps of the area, one dating from 1880, the other from 1974. Children were able to compare the two and to identify certain similarities and differences in buildings, communications and industrial sites. The third clue was a photograph of the old village, now mostly demolished. This enabled the children to develop a knowledge of the

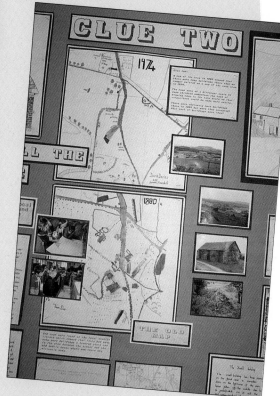

Comparing two maps of the same area but nearly 100 years apart.

98 The method chosen for working was to take the children to the village, give them certain basic information about this former mining community, encourage them to identify questions that might reasonably be investigated and then introduce a series of 'clues' which would ultimately enable the children to develop and use a range of skills and concepts in order to arrive at a series of insights into the experiences and fate of the village.

99 In all, 13 clues were introduced to the children. The first six were presented one after the other in order to allow the children to develop a basic knowledge of the area, the people who had lived there and the lead mining industry. After that, the clues were introduced in response to the researches being carried out by the children and were presented to different groups at different times.

100 The first clue involved the teacher organising a visit to the abandoned mining village and the children paying particular attention to the existence of a former school building. The children were encouraged to pose a question which would prompt historical investigation. The pupils wanted to know: 'Where have all the children gone?' Some details about lead mining in the area were also given at this point.

village as it was and to draw certain conclusions about the changes that had occurred between the village as a working community and its present state. The fourth clue involved a further visit to the village. The children looked at the remains of buildings still visible, examined some of the building materials used and studied and made sketches of the abandoned village school. The fifth clue concerned an exercise in oral history. Children were able to interview some old people who had lived locally and had memories of the mining families of the area. These interviews were transcribed and certain tentative conclusions about work and family life in the village were drawn from them. The

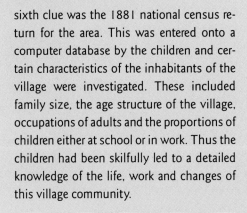

Sketching sites and the remains of buildings as part of the historical investigation.

Churchyards often yield important historical information.

sixth clue was the 1881 national census return for the area. This was entered onto a computer database by the children and certain characteristics of the inhabitants of the village were investigated. These included family size, the age structure of the village, occupations of adults and the proportions of children either at school or in work. Thus the children had been skilfully led to a detailed knowledge of the life, work and changes of this village community.

101 With this basic information and using some of the skills and concepts already developed, the children were then able to use other clues and available resources, deployed by the teacher as required, in order to enquire into those aspects of the history of this village which interested them. For example, the class visited two local churchyards to study headstones giving further information about mortality rates and family structures in the village. The fact that inhabitants of the village were buried in two different parishes led some children to study parochial boundaries in more detail. The County Archivist was invited to the school and she brought original baptismal records which the children entered onto a computer program for later retrieval and anal-

ysis. She was also able to tell the children something of the work of an archivist and to interest them in the range of original documents which are available for local studies. A visit was organised to a local studies library which contained collections of mining journals, some of which gave contemporary accounts of the mine workings in the village being investigated. The pupils were able to use these to gain information about some of the mining techniques and problems present in the mine. Further visits were organised to a local industrial archaeological museum to look at a replica of a similar lead mine and to a lead mining museum, some distance away, which enabled the children to experience something of the prevailing conditions and the hard labour that would be necessary in such mines.

102 This latter experience introduced the children to the process of 'buddling' which is a technique for separating lead ore from other materials through the use of a water sluice. Back at school a group of pupils created such a sluice and were able to demonstrate, using examples of lead ore obtained from the original site, the efficiency of this system for separating rocks and stones of different gravities and

Techniques for separating lead ore – 'buddling' . . .

composition. Another group investigated the efficiency of sieving as a method for separating lead ore.

– and sieving.

The class teacher obtained a collection of lead mining artefacts from a variety of sources. These included explosive-containers, miners' lamps, picks, chains and shovels, all of which would have been used in the local lead mining industry. Children were able to handle these, to record their impressions both visually and in writ-

ten form, and thereby to gain further insights into the working experiences of the lead miners. Finally, a collection of Victorian household artefacts was gathered together in order to help the children develop an imaginative understanding of life in a lead miner's home. For example, the children were able to replicate a Victorian washing day by using contemporary artefacts and wearing appropriate clothing.

'The class teacher obtained a collection of lead mining artefacts . . . explosives-containers, miners' lamps, picks, chains and shovels.'

Thus a wide range of evidence was used by this class to investigate a question of genuine historical interest. Through their enquiry, which lasted for about three-quarters of the school year, the historical skills and concepts outlined above were developed. In addition various other skills were introduced. Children were required to record the results of their investigations using a variety of written forms including factual accounts, imaginative reconstructions, diaries, field notes and tran-

Recording historical findings in three-dimensional form.

scriptions of interviews. They used painting, printing and sketching techniques in order to record their findings in visual form. Information technology was used a great deal to store and analyse complex demographic information. A range of map skills, including reading, interpreting and drawing maps, was developed.

105 In addition to the main historical enquiry, a series of subsidiary investigations was carried out in order to widen the children's experience. For example, the lead which the children had obtained through their various visits was used as a starting-point for a scientific investigation into metals and their properties. This introduced the children to scientific experimentation involving the identification and testing of hypotheses, the notion of fair testing, the control of variables and the drawing of inferences and conclusions.

106 Another investigation concerned the design and construction of a model for the mine headgear that had been used for lowering and raising men to working levels. This involved the making of prototypes and then the building of a working model, based upon a real one that had been restored and placed on a nearby traffic island. This enabled pupils to develop design skills and certain manual skills as they constructed the model out of balsa-wood and, with the help of a parent, to

apply control technology, in order to make the headgear engine work. Finally, drama and music were included within the topic as the children prepared a presentation which involved the dramatic improvisation of an incident which led to the closure of the mine. Thus, as well as developing the central skills and concepts of the enquiry, through the skilful widening and extension of the investigation, the class teacher developed a series of cross-curricular links between the theme and other areas of teaching and learning. The teacher paid considerable attention to the pace of work as she recognised that an enquiry of this range would require considerable efforts by all concerned if tenable and appropriate conclusions were to be reached. She had high expectations of both the children's efforts and the quality of the work they produced. Each child made and filled a workbook detailing his or her activities and the results of their investigations.

Applying control technology to a working model of a mine headgear.

107 The children drafted, re-drafted and edited their written work, either in manuscript or using the word-processing facilities of the microcomputer.

108 In addition they produced class books concerned with a particular aspect of the enquiry. Impressive displays of the 13 clues that had been used in the children's studies enlivened the classroom and stimulated much discussion and enquiry by other children in the school. Each child's progress was monitored by the class teacher through a simple checklist which indicated which areas of investigation had

been begun and completed. None of the work was graded although positive verbal comments were frequently made to the children and positive written comments were sometimes entered into their books. An interesting feature of the work was an evaluation, written by the class teacher, which was entered into the class books as each phase of the investigation was completed. This enabled the children to gain some insight into what they had achieved and where this aspect of the enquiry fitted into the overall research that the class was undertaking.

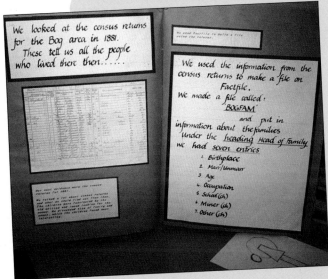

The children produced classbooks at the end of each stage of the investigation.

109 The quality of work produced by the children was high throughout the period of the study. This was due, in part, to the attention that was paid to the question of differentiating activities for the range of abilities within the class. For example the census material was used by some of the less able children to identify one particular family and to thereby produce a visual image of the life and work of this single family using the facts that were known about them. Other children used a much wider range of census material to look for patterns in the information concerning the village and to pose and try to answer certain pertinent questions. For example several inhabitants of the village listed their occupation as 'none'. What this meant, in reality, was investigated, using other sources, by some of the more able children and further categories for the retired, the unemployed and for scholars were identified.

110 Throughout this long, complex and far-ranging investigation the children maintained their interest. Several of the parents were also drawn into the enquiry as they provided additional information or helped with the field trips that the children made. Several parents developed their own interest in the study and took part in some of the investigations, either on their own account or by lending specialist expertise such as with control technology.

111 The reason for the success of this work were as follows:

● the class teacher had a clear idea of the opportunities offered by work of this nature and had strategies for realising these;

● although there was little formal planning of a written kind a great deal of careful preparatory effort was put into the identification and acquisition of relevant and appropriate evidence;

● the work was based upon an original and realistic historical question which the children could identify with and understand;

● throughout the period of the enquiry the teacher maintained a consistent commitment to enquiry-based learning and the development of research skills;

● after the acquisition of certain basic information the children were able to play a part in directing the course of the enquiry and this initiative was supported by the skilful organisation of appropriate resources by the class teacher;

● throughout there was a commitment to a brisk pace and high quality in the work produced and, even though there was little in the way of formal assessment, the children were regularly given information about the progress of their studies and their achievements;

- and, finally, the class teacher made deliberate efforts to maintain interest and coherence in the work through well planned cross-curricular links which enabled the powerful stimulus of this enquiry to be used for the fostering of a wide range of skills in other subject areas.

112 Undoubtedly the children gained a great deal from this work. Their interest had been engaged, they had developed a range of important skills and concepts and had acquired knowledge and understanding which would enable them to adopt a suitably enquiring stance in studies encountered later in their school careers.

CASE STUDY 2

113 The school, with over 200 pupils on roll, is an 'Aided' junior school in a large village. The village has a good range of old and new buildings which can be used for environmental studies. The school building consists of two blocks each of four classrooms linked by a central hall; wherever possible year groups are placed in adjoining classrooms to allow for effective co-operation and use of resources. In the grounds there are features which support the development of topic work through first-hand experience. These include a chequerboard garden and other garden areas, two ponds, a weather centre, hedgerows and an orchard. Sheep, goats, ducks, hens, rabbits and a goose are kept by the school. A nature trail in the school grounds and immediate surroundings is effectively used by the children and an architectural trail has been created in the locality.

114 Resources including maps, slides, charts, pictures and books are generous. There are collections of artefacts for topic work and the museum in the nearest city gives good support. Materials such as logbooks, parish registers and census information from the local archive office are well used.

115 No class teacher has responsibility for topic work throughout the school; the head takes an overall lead. There are, however, teachers with responsibility for geography and history with clear job descriptions which focus attention on their duties. These include leading by example, fostering professional development, establishing relevant aims and objectives, writing guidance material and assessing the effectiveness of the work in the classroom. The job description recognises that in order to carry out these tasks and responsibilities, some non-class contact time must be provided. The availability of this time depends upon prevailing circumstances, but is usually not less than one hour a week.

116 Topic work (history, geography and science) is seen as the central core for the development of all other aspects of the curriculum. Detailed guidelines which identify aims and objectives in history and geography have been produced by the head in full consultation with members of staff. A collegial approach has developed and individual teachers who have responsibilities for aspects of the curriculum give specialist support. Content, concepts and skills were separately identified in the guidelines. Each is given a number and/or letter and this code is used in the teacher's detailed planning notes. For example in a third year junior project 'Man's interaction with his environment' the following concepts and skills are systematically linked to the tasks prepared and the photographs illustrate some of the responses.

G1 To ask geographical questions and develop appropriate vocabulary.
(a) What is this place like?
(b) Where is this place? (in relation to city and fens).
(c) How is this place different to the nearest large city?

G6 To use and develop a range of skills and competencies necessary to carry out geographical enquiry and interpret geographical features.

(g)   Can devise and use a questionnaire.

(i)   Can analyse simple statistics.

A year 4 project included as an aim (G5) 'to develop graphicacy' with the following sub-headings on 'scale'.

G5ii   (a)   Concept of proportion/relative size.

(b)   Scale drawing.

(c)   Need for scale bar on maps.

117   The planning was detailed; skills and ideas were written into the range of activities. The development of resources to support each of the topics was an important element in the work and these were added to from year to year. In the early stages of a topic collections of artefacts and/or natural objects were used to introduce key ideas.

118   The theme in year 5, which has two classes (50 children), was 'Man and his environment'. It sought to integrate all aspects of the curriculum including creative and expressive language. In both classes there were displays which stimulated enquiry; teacher intervention was appropriate and effective. Two children planting seeds in pots were encouraged to consider how the growth of the plants might be recorded. They considered graphs and suggested a format. Groups of children making transects decided through discussion that the vertical scale needed to be exaggerated to show clearly the physical nature of the landscape. The tasks were well differentiated and supported with an expectation that the work would be relevant, interesting and completed to a high standard. For example, two children with learning difficulties discussed photographs of the area and made decisions about the location of the camera and the relationship between the photographs. Another pupil devised his own test to determine the insulating properties of wool and feathers. At the computer three children recorded facts drawn from a variety of graphs.

119   Two more children recorded and compared temperature and rainfall readings from the local area and further afield. They used these findings to establish the reasons for the location of crops.

120   The two classes in year 4 (52 children) combined to work on a well-planned theme 'A comparison of landscapes'. Pictures, books and artefacts were well displayed and contained a variety of questions to be answered.

121   The group work was demanding and built upon previous experience. One group was asked to design a model village and locate it in the best position. They discussed the need for access to water and power and having made the model in card and papier-mâché the children proceeded to map the village and towns.

'One group was asked to design a model village.'

122 Another group used the school grounds to identify the changes in trees, plants, etc. throughout the seasons. Many of their careful observations were recorded in detailed sketches.

123 The village green was used as a focus for work on the different buildings in the village and their history. An imaginative exercise which involved all the children was based on the idea that a property developer had presented plans for the development of the village. Individual pupils played the roles of different people in the village and prepared arguments for or against the proposals, taking into account factors such as pollution dangers, the suitability of existing roads, access to shops and housing needs.

'An imaginative exercise . . . was based on the idea that a property developer had presented ideas for the development of the village.'

124 Topic work in this school was very successful:

• although designed to include all elements of the curriculum there was flexibility in the planning so that some subjects could be developed separately;

• the planning of work was given due regard. The detailed guidelines led to a consistency of approach, organisation and style of learning and provided balance and continuity. Skills and concepts were numbered and hierarchically organised. Using the guidelines and co-operating with other members of staff gave the teachers time and confidence to intervene in the children's learning and guide it forward by the use of skilful questioning;

• each class teacher wrote a termly assessment on the development of topic work for use when the planning guidelines are amended;

• much of the work in the school was based on first-hand experience and investigation;

• visits to the immediate locality and further afield were well planned and effectively used as inspirations for work of quality;

• the children were well motivated and enthusiastic about their learning. The staff had high expectations of all the children and this was reflected in the high standards of work.

CASE STUDY 3

125 This small rural primary school is situated adjacent to the parish church within a village which is itself a rich resource for studies of a geographical and historical nature. The educational potential of the environment is well exploited by the school. Close links with the County Records Office have been developed and local sources such as the National Trust and the Manor House are used regularly. The school population reflects the broad social and economic mix of the village, the majority of its 75 pupils having relatively advantaged family backgrounds. There is sufficient space in the old main building, which includes the former school house, for a reference library and resources room. In addition there are two modern demountable classrooms.

126 The head takes an enthusiastic lead in the development of environmental studies work throughout the school and he has considerable expertise in the historical and geographical aspects. Although he does not teach alongside his two colleagues, he comments upon their plans and displays a sound grasp of the teaching and learning processes evident within these older two classes. The good practice which exists in his own class and that of his deputy provides an effective model which has a beneficial influence upon the quality of work within the third class, thus helping to achieve consistently good standards throughout the school.

127 The guidelines for this area of the curriculum are of good quality and clearly indicate those skills, attitudes and concepts it is hoped will be developed through environmental studies over the seven-year period children attend the school. This document, produced jointly by the head and staff, identifies three stages of development within each of the suggested themes. These stages correspond broadly with the three age ranges represented in the classes and help towards promoting progression in the work. Class teachers use the guideline topics as the foundation for their planning and add other experiences where appropriate. It is expected that environmental studies will occupy approximately one-quarter of the timetable, but this includes subjects other than history and geography, the emphasis depending upon the nature of the particular topic. This generous time allocation reflects the priority given to this aspect of the curriculum.

128 Resource provision is very good and extensive use is made of primary source materials including photographs, tithe maps and a varied collection of photocopied documents, mainly inventories, diary extracts, census returns and drawings. There are also examples of children's work in written, pictorial and three-dimensional form which have been kept as a reference resource for use by future pupils. The school has a policy statement for the use of the computer. Effective use of information technology is seen as one way of reinforcing the topics studied.

129 Year 2 and year 3 pupils were studying their village. One of the lessons involved an exploration of the children's perceptions of the village layout and location introduced through drama in the small hall. The teacher had brought a number of envelopes which contained clues about a specific place in the village which the children were to visit. These were cut-out pieces of a small-scale map which fitted together like a jigsaw. The teacher acted the role of a stranger to the village whose uncle had just died and left the envelopes of clues in his belongings. The clues were portrayed as secrets and all the children swore to secrecy by Cubs' or Brownies' honour and other 'oaths'. This was all taken very seriously and discussion proceeded about how the clues might best be interpreted.

130 The class divided into five groups and each group was given an envelope of clues. The children proceeded to attempt to interpret these; there was a lot of discussion and excitement. In the classroom, the groups were able to fit together the pieces of the map. They then found that the red letters written on each map made up the word 'troll'. The children realised that the place they must go to was the so-called Trip Trap bridge in the village.

131 A walk was organised to the bridge. At several points on the way, the children stopped and drew details of their route on a sketch map. These maps were of good quality and in many cases showed a clear understanding of orientation and scale. Each group was expected to refer to its jigsaw map and to mark each stopping-point. Eventually at the 'Troll' bridge the children found a box containing a facsimile of an old document on which was written an

Studying the gravestone of a boy who died 'in uncertain circumstances'.

inscription from a gravestone. This generated further excitement and speculation as to what it could mean. The next stage involved a search in the churchyard for the gravestone concerned; that of a boy who died at the age of 10 in 1912 in uncertain circumstances.

132   This lesson was an example of how drama could be used to generate a sense of excitement and mystery within class investigations. There were clear historical and geographical outcomes to these imaginative and well-planned experiences which were based on the belief that children should be given responsibilities and opportunities for independent thought.

133   The project for pupils in years 4, 5 and 6 was on the village churchyard. There were several inter-related studies in progress, all of which involved the use of primary evidence:

• a survey of the gravestones using a video-tape made by the children which showed every stone. Each one was given a number. Two children were working through this video recording marking the location of the stones on a small plan of the graveyard;

• four children were in the churchyard with an ancillary helper, recording data from a number of gravestones for inclusion on the date base. This involved measuring and making decisions about shape, classifications, decoration and details about the people buried;

• the classification of the gravestones using an information outline sheet developed by the Manpower Services Commission and the Department of Archaeology at a local university. Two children were putting this information onto a computer data base program which was later to be interrogated by them. The aim was to see if a pattern could be found that would link headstone style with, among other things, the date of the burial;

• two children were using reference books to research the ways in which other cultures deal with their dead. They were looking at Hindu methods of cremation and beliefs about the body and the soul. The children's research techniques and higher order reading skills were well developed;

• a group of four children was using a photocopy of the 1841 national census return for the village and was copying out its information after deciphering its somewhat difficult writing. Their next task was to format the data base on the computer and enter this information for analysis. Interesting discussion took place on the interpretation of some words, and other documents from the period were used to identify the shape of the letter 'S', as written in copper-plate, circa 1850;

• three children were looking at a photocopy of a marriage certificate dated 1820. They wrote a letter to a friend in which they imagined they were guests at the wedding ceremony and described what took place, on the basis of the available evidence. The subsequent assignment was to write a newspaper article using a computer program;

- three children were researching a report written in the nineteenth century about some people from the village who emigrated to Canada. This included a map of their route to the port of Bristol and of the route to Canada.

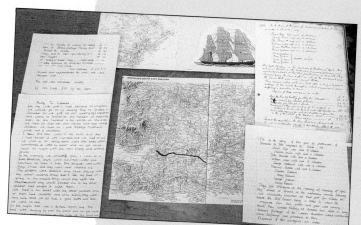

Investigating the story of villagers who emigrated to Canada in the nineteenth century.

134 This lesson was characterised by a good balance of historical and geographical activities, a strong emphasis on the acquisition of skills, and a clear understanding of the knowledge to be acquired. The children worked successfully and responsibly in small groups. Their abilities to interpret evidence, seek explanations and solve problems were particularly well developed.

135 The teaching methods and learning outcomes in the school had many sound features:

- well-planned first-hand experiences, well-paced work and an emphasis on developing skills and concepts through relevant and challenging tasks which the pupils were encouraged to organise for themselves including working collaboratively in groups;

- books and resources were easily accessible and regularly used by the children;

- as the children moved up through the school there was an increasing emphasis on sustained work;

- pupils were engaged in a good deal of research involving, for example, the use of primary sources to look for clues and to establish an evidence base for recording and processing data obtained during the investigation. Through such activities the children learned some of the skills and techniques employed by historians and geographers;

- although little in the way of formal assessment was undertaken, the teachers were aware of the quality of the work produced;

- there were strong cross-curricular links which gave both relevance and purpose to the acquisition of a wide range of skills and knowledge;

- the enlisting of voluntary help from parents made a valuable contribution to practical activities and field work;

- classrooms were organised into work areas for specific activities, to allow children to engage in practical tasks without disturbing their peers who were pursuing different types of assignments.

Aspects of Primary Education series

The education of children under five
HMSO, 1989. £3.50 ISBN 0 11 270670 3

*The teaching and learning of
mathematics*
HMSO, 1989. £4.95 ISBN 0 11 270687 8

*The teaching and learning of
science*
HMSO, 1989. £3.95 ISBN 0 11 270694 0

Printed in the United Kingdom for Her Majesty's Stationery Office
Dd 289094 C90 10/89 25038